Luck, I don't think so!!!

Marla Almaraz

WestBow
PRESS
A DIVISION OF THOMAS NELSON

WestBow Press books may be ordered through booksellers or by contacting:

WestBow Press
A Division of Thomas Nelson
1663 Liberty Drive
Bloomington, IN 47403
www.westbowpress.com
1-(866) 928-1240

ISBN: 978-1-4497-2873-1 (sc)
ISBN: 978-1-4497-2872-4 (e)
Library of Congress Control Number: 2011918274
Printed in the United States of America
WestBow Press rev. date: 10/19/2011

Contents

Introduction

In the following pages, I know that I am disclosing many personal details about my life. At first I was afraid to expose them because of the ramifications and being condemned by others. But the words I found in the Bible kept me moving forward. **In John 15:18, Jesus says,** *"If the world hates you, you know that it hated me first."*

My main purpose for writing this testimony is to show you that an ordinary person like me can be an example of what God can do for you if you just give your life to him. I also want to try to prevent at least one person from taking the path of destruction that I chose.

*So if just **one** person gives his or her life to Christ by reading this testimony, I have accomplished what I have set out to do, and **all** of heaven will rejoice!*
"All the glory goes to God Almighty."

(1 Corinthians 14:31) *"For you all can prophesy one by one, that all may learn and may be encouraged."*

(Romans 14:8) *"For if we live, we live to the Lord; and if we die, we die to the Lord; therefore, whether we live or die, we are the Lord's.*

1. Jesus/God Lives

First of all, if you do not believe that there is a God, I hope my story will change your mind. He most definitely does exist, and he lives. I also believe that that God plans and sets the stage for everyone to have an opportunity to accept Jesus Christ as his or her personal Savior. It is up to you how it turns out!

The events that have occurred in my life were not just coincidences that happened by chance or luck. My heavenly Father had his hands in all of them. God set the time and date for our appointment to meet, and you will read how it turned out for me. All of the testimonies that I have written about are to give honor and glory to God.

You see, *we* do not pick God; *he* picks us. This is found in almost every book of the New Testament, but I decided to only list the two Scriptures from the Gospel of John.

When God draws us to him, it is in a very distinct way. It is usually surrounded by a tragedy that *does not* happen and you know down deep inside that it was a blessing from God. However most people just pass it off and acknowledge it as good luck and go on with their life as though nothing has happened. This is the tragedy, because even though our loving God is very patient with us in trying to get our attention, if we have such a hardened heart that he can't penetrate it, he will eventually move on.

Marla Almaraz

(John: 6:44) *"No one can come to me unless the Father who sent me draws him; and I raise up at the last day."*

(John: 15:16) *" For you did not choose me, but I chose you and appointed that you should go and bear fruit, and that your fruit should remain, that whatever you ask the Father in my name He may give you."*

2. We Can Have a Personal Relationship with God

Most people don't realize that God wants to have a personal relationship with us. They treat God like he is a distant entity. What is even worse—most people don't even believe that he even exists these days. They can't conceive that God created us for company and wants to love us, bless us, and take care of us. You see, God wants us to love him without being forced to, so he gave us our own mind and will.

From the Scriptures below, you can see that our Lord God has feelings too, just like us. He is happy, loving, and enjoys blessing us. But you can also see that we hurt him and anger him in the way we treat him. He is the holy God that made this world for us and gave us life. *We just can't ever forget that.* He deserves to be honored and praised.

Scriptures of God's Happiness with Blessings

(Genesis 1:27)—"So God created man in His own image: in the image of God He created him; male and female He created them."

(Genesis 1:28)—"Then God blessed them, and God said to them, 'Be fruitful and multiply; fill the earth and subdue it; have

dominion over the fish of the sea, over the birds of the air, and over every living thing that moves on earth.'"

(Genesis 2:7)—*"And the Lord God formed man of the dust of the ground, and breathed into his nostrils the breath of life; and man became a living being."*

Scriptures of God's Sadness and Anger

(Genesis 6:5)—*"The Lord saw that the wickedness of man was great in the earth, and that every intent of the thoughts of his heart was only evil continually."*

(Genesis 6:6)—*"And the Lord was sorry that He had made man on the earth, and he grieved in His heart."*

(Genesis 6:7)—*"So the Lord said, 'I will destroy man whom I have created from the face of the earth, both man and beast, creeping thing and birds of the air, for I am sorry that I made them.'"*

3. My Divine Appointment

I have started my testimony almost like an autobiography because the Lord drew me to him at a very early age. As you read on, you will see that if the Lord had not intervened in my life, I might never have known Christ at all.

I grew up in a rather large family, with four brothers and one sister. We lived in an old, remodeled house that was once an army barracks. It was located on a private dirt road in a small, quaint neighborhood out in the country. Our family was very poor, and we learned early in life to do without. My two older brothers and I were born within two years of each other and were very close, while my two younger brothers and sister came along about six years later.

Our dad, a Swedish man, worked very hard as a delivery driver for a local lumberyard, making minimum wage, so it was a constant struggle to try and support us. My mother, a Danish woman stayed at home raising the six of us.

Even though we were poor, my dad always managed to provide us with enough food to eat. Clothing was a different story. Every summer, my two older brothers and I would have to pick bush berries down the street from our house in order to earn enough money to buy our school clothes.

I was pretty happy living in this small neighborhood because the neighbors were all very close and everyone watched out for each other. However, there was one small problem: there weren't any girls my age to play with, so I usually had to play by myself. My brothers had their friends, so sometimes I would play with them, but most of the time I was alone, so I became a loner early on.

Then one day, all of that changed. Some people came to look at the vacant house next to ours, and I couldn't believe my eyes when two young girls got out the car. I was very excited, because one of those girls seemed to be pretty close to my age. ***So just as God had planned it, they moved in.***

A couple of days after they moved in, I needed to figure out a way of meeting them, so I threw a ball over the fence. When I went to retrieve it, I introduced myself to Janet and Angie. Janet was around my age, five years old, and Angie was eleven. Janet and I became best friends almost instantly. At last I had someone to play dolls with!

I soon found myself wanting to spend every waking moment at their house because the atmosphere there was so warm and loving. This was very different from what I was used to. In our home, there seemed to be continuous arguing, fighting, and utter chaos. My dad would drink, my older brothers cussed, and my mom was unhappy most of the time because of it. So to see an entire family showing love, respect, and truly caring for one another was beautiful. I wished my family could be like this too!

One Sunday, Janet invited me to go to church with them, and I really liked it. So I started attending church every Sunday from that day forward. In Sunday school, I learned of God's power and his love for us. There were three miracles that God performed that have stuck in my mind to this very day. One was when God helped Moses part the Red Sea so the people of Israel could escape the torture and slavery of the Egyptians **(Exodus 14:21–31)**. In another, Daniel escaped certain death when the king threw him into the lions' den, because God shut the mouths of the lions **(Daniel 6:16–23)**. And lastly, how Jonah survived being swallowed by a big fish and how God had caused the fish to vomit him out **(Jonah 1:17–2:10)**. After learning about these, I realized that there was a lot more depth to God than just the Ten Commandments that my mom had taught me about.

My mom had a somewhat religious background, so we had a copy of the Ten Commandments in a wooden frame hanging on the wall in our kitchen. Each time we were naughty, she would remind us that we were breaking God's laws and he would punish us. But I learned the most important thing of all by far, why Jesus Christ came to earth and how he died on the cross for our sins so we could go to heaven. When I heard this, I could not believe it. Jesus died for me! I felt so sad.

As the years went by, I became more and more knowledgeable about the books of the Bible and all of the miracles Jesus performed—walking on water, making the blind see, bringing the dead to life. But the most important thing I learned was the **grace of God.** God's grace is free for the asking, and this meant if you confessed your sins and asked Jesus to come into your life, you would be in God's grace and have everlasting life. **John 3:16 says,** *"For God so loved the world that he gave his only begotten son, that whosoever believes Him should not perish but have everlasting life."* Boy! This was very powerful to me and seemed to be such a respectable and easy thing to do in comparison to what Jesus has done for me.

One Sunday morning before the close of the service, the pastor asked, "If anyone wants to come up and ask Jesus to forgive them of their sins and receive him as their personal Savior, please come to the altar, and I will pray and lay hands on you."

With Janet's encouragement, I walked up to the front of the church, and she came to stand beside me.

As the pastor started praying over me, I began sobbing and asking the Lord to forgive me of my sins and come into my heart. When the pastor finished, I knew that I was saved, not only because of the way I felt inside, but because it is promised in the Bible, and God does not break promises. When I went back to my seat, I felt very happy because I had poured out my heart to Jesus and felt cleansed and pure.

The following Sunday, Janet and I were both water baptized in front of the entire congregation, and I knew that my destiny was heaven. Janet's mother explained to me, "There is one more thing that needs to happen before you can go to heaven: you have to be born again."

I was not quite sure what Janet's mom meant about being "born again" and receiving the "Holy Spirit," so I found it in the Bible in the book of **Acts 2:38.** *"Repent, and let everyone of you be baptized in the name of Jesus Christ for the remissions of your sins; and you shall receive the gift of the Holy Spirit."* I also found it in **John 3:3.** *"Most assuredly, I say to you, unless one is born again, he cannot see the Kingdom of God."*

Several months passed, and then one Sunday evening, as I sat on the pew listening to the pastor's message, something happened to me. The pastor said, "If anyone wants to come up to the Altar for a special anointing and have me lay hands on them, please come forward."

Suddenly I felt a force that literally drew me out of my seat and to the front of the church. As the pastor prayed over me and put his hand on my head, I began to pray to Jesus from the bottom of my heart and thanked him for loving me and giving salvation. All of a sudden, I felt a warm and loving presence filling my entire body. It was something I had never experienced before. I became completely oblivious that I was in front of the entire congregation and began talking in a language that was unknown to me. I felt like my entire body was lit up like a 150-watt light bulb and someone had taken a toothbrush and scrubbed the inside of my body clean, leaving it as white as snow. I remained in this state, completely focused on Jesus and unaware of my surroundings for about ten minutes.

Finally, when I turned around, I saw all of the church members clapping and praising Jesus with shouts of joy. I knew that had been filled with the Holy Spirit. I felt completely different and have never felt so much love and warmth extending out my body in my entire life.

That night when I came home from church, I felt the need to try to change every member in my family. Even though I was only nine years old, I knew that my family needed to have Christ in their lives, and it was up to me to try to do it. So I shared my experience with my two older brothers first and explained that they needed to give their life to Christ. They said, "You're crazy."

When I told my mom what had happened, she just listened and seemed to be very happy and said, "I believe in God, honey, and that is why I have the Ten Commandments hanging on the kitchen wall. I just can't make it to church every Sunday because of the babies."

However, when I told my dad, he said, "I don't know why you even bother going to church, because only the Jews are going to go to heaven!"

This really bothered me, and I had to find if there was any truth to this. It did not seem right, especially after the way I felt inside. So I asked the pastor to find out if what my dad had told me was true. The pastor said, "When Christ died for us on the cross, it was a new covenant, and it opened the way for *everyone* that believed in Jesus, confessed their sins, and received him as their personal savior, would go to heaven."

After hearing this from the pastor, I was very relieved. So with this confirmation, I began trying to act just like Christ did and prayed every day for guidance. It began to change my way of thinking.

4. The Spirit of God Changes the Way You Think

On my first day back to school after receiving the Holy Spirit, I wanted to distance myself from my other classmates. I wanted to start practicing what I was learning in Sunday school, so I did not want to act like them or try to fit in anymore. Well, for some reason, this really bothered one girl in my class. Even though we were really never very close or even played together, she seemed to make it her mission to hurt me **in** any way she could. Every time I encountered her, she physically hurt me. She would hit me, push me down, and grip and twist my fingers backward to the point of severe pain. But instead of calling her names and fighting back, I asked myself, *What would Jesus do and say in this very situation?* so I tried putting his methods into practice. I also remembered reading in the Bible what it says about revenge. It is found in **Romans 12:19: "Vengeance is Mine, I will repay, says the Lord."** So I held my tongue and asked her, "Why are you doing this to me? I have done nothing to you." I also said, "No matter what you do, I will not hate you."

Well, guess what: it works! The very next day, this girl came up to me and said, "You're weird," and continued, "How can you be so nice?" When I told her that I was trying to do what Jesus wants me to do, she just stood there in silence and walked away. The following day, she came up to me again and apologized for what she had been doing to me and wanted to be my friend. I said, "Yes," so we started playing together. She wanted to hear more about Jesus, so I began teaching her what I was learning in Sunday school. We ended up being very close friends.

5. A Sister from God

Around this same time, my dad announced that Mom was pregnant. I was very happy and began praying daily for a sister, because I absolutely did not want another brother.

So on January 14, 1964, my dad came home from the hospital and announced that I had a baby sister named Cheryl. No matter what anyone says, I know that God had heard my prayers and answered them. Although I was eleven years older and there was a huge age difference between us, I did not care. I enjoyed helping my mom take care of her, and Cheryl and I became very close.

6. Divorce and Death—My Downward Spiral Begins

As the years passed and I hit my teenage years, I started to drift away from the church. The Christian neighbors ended up moving away, and the pastor died. Janet could see me drifting away from God, and she was concerned. So one day before she moved, she came to me and said, "Marla no matter what happens in your life, you will always know your way back home." I had no idea what she meant at that time, but I would soon find out.

After Janet moved—and without the encouragement of her family to keep me on the straight and narrow—I ended up turning my focus to a neighborhood boy named Ron. We started dating, and one thing led to another. I ended up pregnant at the age of sixteen with my daughter. Ron and I married, and everything seemed to be going pretty well for at least six years.

It wasn't until after my second child, Steve, that I found out that Ron was cheating on me. This was one of the most painful things I have ever endured. I was not only losing my husband, but losing Ron was like losing my best friend too! I actually did not want to live anymore. I knew that according to the Bible, God unites you in marriage, and it is supposed to last "until death do you part."

So I sought biblical advice from a Baptist pastor in town as to what I should do.

He explained to me that adultery is not acceptable in God's eyes, and if we could not reconcile, it would not be a sin to divorce. So to sum it all, up we divorced.

On December 7, 1971, I lost my dad to cirrhosis of the liver. Before he died, he said, "I had a dream last night which showed me six coffins, and one was filled." Then he continued, saying, "One of my children will not reach the age of eighteen." This really scared all of us who were still under that age. In fact, as each of us reached our eighteenth birthday, there was a sigh of relief. The only one left was Cheryl.

Several years passed, and Cheryl had grown up into a beautiful young lady. She was fourteen years old, and I can still remember like it was yesterday, the day I received that horrible call from my baby brother Chuck. He said there had been a head-on collision on Freedom Boulevard and Cheryl had been pronounced dead. The doctors at Watsonville Hospital rushed her to the Dominican Hospital because it had better facilities to treat trauma and head injuries like hers. They tried to revive her, but her head had been so crushed that she went into a coma and was being kept alive only by life support.

Finally, after three days, we had to make a decision about keeping her on life support, because we could not afford to leave it on indefinitely. So once the life support was turned off, my entire family gathered at my house, and we began praying. We knew that whatever was going to happen was God's will. On January 1, 1976, the hospital called and said that Cheryl had died. The Lord had taken her home. This was devastating for our whole family, but especially hard for my mom, because it is hard to lose one of your babies. It was then that I knew how God must have felt to lose his only Son.

Losing my dad, my sister, having my best friend move, losing the pastor, and going through a divorce sent me into a frenzy of drinking to drown out the pain. At this point, I turned my back on God and began my downhill spiral.

7. Backsliding

After losing these loved ones, I proceeded to raise my daughter and son by myself. I was able to stay in the house Ron and I had bought together because there wasn't enough equity at that time of our divorce to fight over. So he took the new car and signed the house over to me. This sounds great, doesn't it? However, I had no job skills whatsoever except picking strawberries. I did not know how I would be able to make the monthly payments, fix the roof, and build the retaining wall that was desperately needed to resolve the water issues with the property's landscape.

Luckily, I found work, with the help of a friend at an electronics company, who was willing to train me. They paid minimum wage, and there were no medical or dental benefits offered, so I had to seek help from welfare and try as best I could to make that monthly house payment. I was really struggling to make ends meet.

Even though I did not really have the money to spare, I continued in a frenzy of drinking and partying to drown out the pain. I relied on my mother for childcare and financial assistance to keep me afloat. Finally, on July 9, 1979, I found a job with another electronics company, and my whole world changed. This company paid well and had excellent medical and dental benefits that began the first day of employment. This enabled me to finally get off of welfare and food stamps. For the first time in years, I was able to buy food, build up my savings, and make my house payment without any problems.

Then on July 7, 1980, my house caught on fire. Just three days after the Fourth of July, my seven-year-old son had found a book of matches, took a pair of his pajamas out of his dresser drawers and hid in his closet and lit them on fire because he wanted to see if his pajamas were fire retardant. Well, they weren't. This fire completely destroyed his room, the hallway, and parts of the kitchen and living room. The entire house had severe smoke damage, and everything I had was destroyed in less than twenty minutes.

I did not know what to do. I sought guidance from my manager at work to help me with my insurance claim, because he had just recently gone through this. With his help, I was able to select the contractor I wanted, the house was completely remodeled, and I even had enough money to purchase all new furniture.

Within a week after the fire, I was able to cash in on a stock option from my job at Tandem Computers that allowed me to buy a new car.

At the time this was all taking place, I just did what needed to be done. It was not until after everything was over that I realized that this was a blessing in disguise from God.

Even though I had backslidden from my Christian walk, God never left me. God saw my struggles and sent this miracle to wake me up. Just think: God took care of everything that was wrong with the house and my financial circumstances within three months' time. Isn't that amazing? Once I realized this, I began to go back to church and give thanks to God for what he had done for me, because I did not deserve it. He is amazing and forgiving.

8. When Your Children Know the Lord

I was around twenty-five years of age, still single, and determined to raise my two kids with the knowledge of God, the way I was taught. So I started taking them to church. One specific incident made me very glad that I had taken my daughter to church. Once my daughter learned that God was the ultimate boss and had the fear of God's judgment when you disobey, it made it easier to discipline her.

When my daughter was around fifteen years old, she came to me one day and asked if she could go to Los Angeles with some friends of hers. I asked her if there were going to be any boys going on this trip, and she said, "No! Mom, there will not be any boys."

Well, I knew by her facial expressions that this was a lie, so with the wisdom of the Holy Spirit inside me, I pointed up to heaven and I said, "Well, if God says you can go, then I say you can go." Guess what happened? My daughter said, "Oh, Mom! I can't go," and she did not go.

I did not have to do anything, because she knew that God had the final word. This was the easiest decision that I ever had to make in my life, because I gave it to the pro.

9. My Life Starts Falling Apart

You would think that after seeing God in action with the house fire and how easy it was to delegate a difficult decision to him regarding my daughter, I would have learned, but I didn't. Instead I started to drift into a sinful lifestyle again, which included drinking, partying, and one boyfriend after another. This went on for the next five years. I was financially set, my house almost paid in full, and I did not need God, *I thought*.

It was around age thirty that I became very lonely for a soul mate and had an uncontrollable desire to have more children. I was still employed at Tandem and had a nice little nest egg set aside, so I could easily afford to bring a new husband and more children into our household. So one night at a night club, I met a man named Casey, and we hit if off. We dated for several months, and when I learned that I was pregnant, we got married. That was in 1983, and my son, Adrian, was born in March of 1984. Then, eighteen months later, I gave birth to another son, Evan. Now I felt complete.

However, it was after having these last two children that things began to fall apart, because with this small three-bedroom house, I had no choice but to borrow on the equity to add another bedroom. In the meantime, I had quit my job because it became too costly to pay for childcare and just too hard to work with two small children, period. So we really began to struggle trying to make ends meet and living on one income, which was only around $800 a month.

Finally, my oldest brother helped my husband get a job working for a very reputable company. At first this job was only part-time, but it eventually became permanent. I went back to work, and our financial problems began to even out somewhat. Things were going okay, at least for the first two years, until we started having arguments on how to raise the boys.

My husband was six years younger than me, and these were his only children. But I had ten years of experience raising my daughter and son by myself, and it seemed like all I was doing was teaching him what not to do in the discipline department.

This constant arguing continued to the point where I decided I could not take it anymore. I explained to my husband, "I do not want to waste the rest of my life arguing with you. I want a divorce."

We had a lengthy and expensive divorce, and I felt very lucky that he did not get any portion of the equity in the house. Later in life, I realized that this was one of the biggest mistakes I ever made, because my ex-husband was a good man who never would have cheated on me. And worst of all, I had no right to divorce him in God's eyes. I was the one who was going to face God's judgment for causing my ex-husband to commit adultery by remarrying another woman out of loneliness.

As you keep reading, you will find that it is ironic that all of the fighting and all of the money I spent on attorney's fees to keep from losing my house were fruitless. Little did I know that with the path I was on, God was going to allow the Devil to take it away from me anyway!

10. Running with the Devil!

There I was, single and raising four children by myself again! Luckily, I still had my job at SCI, because Tandem had sold out to them, so I was financially okay. With this in place, I continued to drink and party and did not even consider thanking the Lord for being able to keep my house, for having four healthy children, and for my dependable job. I thought that I did not need God, because I thought that I had my life completely under control and everything was going great!

Then, all of a sudden, on February 28, 1999, SCI announced that it was closing the plant. So on April 1, 1999, I lost my job. I felt that the rug had been pulled out from under me.

Now in the midst of all this, I had met another man named Jessie and allowed him to move in with me. My children and my brothers did not like him and warned me, "He is just using you." They tried to make me understand that I needed to get rid of him. They said, "He is a loser." He had been in prison, and for some reason, I felt the need to help him get back on his feet. So instead of listening to my family, I took his side and actually distanced myself from my family and continued on my downward spiral.

So now I was around forty years old and on unemployment, which wasn't much, so I ended up using my credit cards to buy food and, of course, his drugs. Jessie is the one who introduced cocain to me, and our entire relationship was one big party after another.

I found myself using my credit cards daily for cash withdrawals in order to keep him happy. Jessie was abusive and controlling, and the only way to keep him from beating me was to buy him his drugs. During this miserable seven-year relationship with Jessie, I lost my mother to a heart attack. She was my rock, and I felt empty without her.

Soon after her death, I received my inheritance and paid off the balance I owed on my house. I thought that I was set. But I ended up having to borrow almost the same amount of money that I had received from my inheritance on an equity loan to pay off the continually increasing credit card debts.

11. My Downward Spiral Continues

Finally I had no choice but to sell the house to pay off all my creditors. After the sale of the house, I had enough money to buy a house in a small, desolate town outside of Los Banos, so Jessie and I moved up there.

My son, Adrian, who hated Jessie, joined the marines, and Evan moved in with my daughter. As for Jessie and me, we continued to party at the new house.

At the new house, the money that was left was dwindling fast. How could I have known that this town is what I would consider the drug capital of the world? In this desolate, tiny, depressed town, you could find drugs around every corner. In fact, every other house had what you wanted.

I went through complete hell with Jessie. I wanted so many times to get rid of him now because I grew to hate him. His daily hunger for drugs was breaking me. But when I said I wanted him to leave, he would threaten me by saying, "If I can't have you, no one else will either. I'll hurt anyone you try to have a relationship with. "

He was controlling and would hide my cell phone from me so that I could not make contact with my family for help. I was literally trapped by this maniac! He would beat me daily if I did not buy him his drugs. Many times I would actually catch him in bed with other women right inside the house, but I could not do anything about it. I guess at this point, I was actually relieved, because we were not sleeping together at all, so at least these other women were keeping him satisfied and away from me.

I began to hate myself and everything I had done, because I too had become a victim of this drug addiction. It seemed that my whole day consisted of trying to find enough money to purchase the drugs we needed for that day. There is a song called "Running with the Devil." This is exactly what I was doing.

Even though I used my credit cards for cash withdrawals, I was keeping track of them. I could not figure out why my credit card debts that I had just paid off with the sale of my house had gotten out of control again. But later I found out that Jessie had been taking my credit cards to make cash withdrawals while I was asleep. He had found the secret place where I had hidden my passwords. So with the debts so large again, I had no choice but to put this new house on the market to sell too.

I didn't know that the real estate broker I selected to sell my house in this town was crooked and had convinced me to become a second-mortgager. He gave me one half of the sale price up front and wrote up a thirty-year note for the balance, in which I would be receiving monthly payments for thirty years.

So with the up-front cash, I purchased an older motor home and packed up whatever I could fit into it and sold everything else. Sadly, most of the money we got from the yard sales of my household items always went for more drugs.

At this point, I realized that turning away from God had led to this. Everything I had worked so hard for the last thirty years was gone. My excellent credit was completely shot. Thirty years of hard work completely down the drain in less than seven years.

12. A Message from God

I must mention that even though I had backslidden and was not living like a Christian should, I still belonged to God. I asked Jesus Christ to come into my heart at the age of nine, so from that day forward, I was a child of God. He doesn't want his sheep to remain lost, so he sends you messages or messengers to remind you that it is time to come home.

One afternoon, as Jessie and I sat in the motor home, which was parked in the main shopping center of the little town, literally starving because all of the money had been spent on drugs, there was a knock at the door. When Jessie opened the door, a lady handed him a bag of food. As the lady walked off, Jessie said to me, "Who was that?"

I said, "I don't know. I have never seen her before." Then instantly I knew that God must have sent her, because who else in this town knew how hungry we were or even cared?

I got up and ran out of the motor home and caught up to that lady. I was crying, and I hugged her with all of my might and I said, "Thank you so much."

She said, "Honey, we have a bakery shop right here in the shopping center, and we have been watching you for quite a while." She continued, "You do not belong with this type of man, and you need to get away from him. We will help you in any way we can."

This was a messenger sent directly from the Lord, and I knew it. So I planned my escape.

13. First Plan for Escape and God Rescues Me

The next day, I decided to try to break free from Jessie. While he was asleep inside the motor home, I snuck out, took the Kia, and drove to Watsonville. I made it over Pacheco Pass but ran out of gas on the shortcut to Gilroy. This was very scary, because I was a woman by myself on a small dirt road in the middle of nowhere, tucked between two orchards, and it was getting dark. The closest gas station was about ten miles away, and with my bad hip, I could not walk that far. I did not know what to do.

I saw headlights in the distance and stood in the middle of the dirt road, waving my hands, yelling, "Help!" But the car just passed by, and I felt completely lost and helpless. Then I noticed backup lights, and a spark of hope filled my heart. As the car turned around and headed back in my direction and got closer, I yelled, "Please help me, I ran out of gas."

Then I heard a very familiar voice coming from inside the car saying, "Mom, is that you?" I could not believe my ears. What were the chances that Evan would have come looking for me on this particular night and especially on this dirt road? Well, I know why! It was not by chance that my son came to my rescue; the Lord had sent him.

Evan had been telling his sister all day that he was going to go looking for me, and she had told him, "Just forget it, because you will never find her."

But my son explained to me, "I kept hearing a little voice in my head that kept saying, *Go look for your mom.*" He said that this voice became very strong and he had to go. Thank God my son listened and did what this voice directed him to do, because I don't know what would have happened to me if he hadn't.

Once Evan and I were back in Watsonville, we both realized that the voice he had heard was God. We just sat in his car in complete awe because we had both witnessed God in action.

As we sat, I divulged my plans to leave Jessie. He was very happy and said, "I will help you, Mom." So I headed back to the motor home, which was parked in the shopping center of this small town, with my plan to break away for good.

14. Slim Escape from a Murderer

Once I was back at the motor home, I began to put together my plan to get away from Jessie once and for all. We were sitting in the motor home, parked inside the shopping center, and Jessie had just finished the last of his drugs. He began to get upset and said to me, "I want to get more."

I said, "No, we don't have any more money."

He became furious and broke a beer bottle on the corner of the counter and came at me with the jagged edge. He said, "I know you have more money, and I know that you have drugs hidden somewhere in here, and if you don't give them to me right now, I am going to break your neck" I could not convince him otherwise, and I could see it in his eyes that he was serious about breaking my neck because I have never seen eyes like this before in my life. They were cold and glassy and I knew they were the eyes of a person that had snapped.

So I got up and ran out of that motor home as fast as my feet would carry me. I kept running down the street because Jessie was chasing me, but I noticed that he stopped because a police car was pulling up beside me.

The officer said, "What is wrong?"

I said, "My boyfriend just threatened to beat me, so I am going to walk to Watsonville."

The officer just looked at me with disgust and said, "You can't walk to Watsonville from here it's over 150 miles away."

I said, "Just watch me." I was determined to get away from **Jessie.**

Finally the officer said, "I should take you to jail for being under the influence of drugs, but I think you need help more than jail time, so get in, and we will try to get you some help."

So they took me to a shelter in Merced, where I remained for two weeks.

15. Final Escape Complete

During this time, I had time to straighten up and plan my final escape from Jessie. The shelter would not allow me to leave unless someone came for me, so my daughter and her husband came to pick me up. They drove me to the parking lot to get the motor home, and I drove it to Watsonville. I parked it behind their house so that it was hidden and Jessie would not be able to find me.

Now that I was in the motor home, safely parked behind my daughter's house, I was finally able to set up a plan for how to pay off all of my creditors and get my life back on track.

The first thing I needed to do was to sue that crooked real estate agent for setting me up in an illegal contract called a thirty-year note as a second mortgagor. This was totally illegal. The attorney I hired helped me break this contract, and because this Realtor did not even have a license to sell properties in the first place, it gave me even more ground to stand on. So because of what this Realtor did and the fact that he did not have a Realtor's license, I won the case hands down and ended up getting the entire amount of the note, which was around $60,000.

I can only thank God for intervening in this, because that crooked Realtor and his illegal contract was actually a safe haven for my money at that time or I might have otherwise lost all of it to drugs.

So the good Lord was watching over me and turned what was bad into good.

Romans 8:28: "And we know that all things work together for good to those who love God, to those who are called to his purpose."

16. I Came Home to Christ

At forty-six years old, I had lost everything that I owned. With what little money I had managed to keep, I negotiated an agreed payoff amount with each creditor one by one, until I was debt-free. However, even with these negotiated credit card payoffs, my credit was still shot, so I had to pay cash for everything.

I was able to purchase a used older Honda and still had enough cash live on for about a year.

Do you see what happens to your life when think that you are so high and mighty and forget your Lord?

One night, while sitting in the motor home, parked behind my daughter's house, I started thinking of what a complete mess I had made of my life. My family had pretty much deserted me, and I had nowhere else to turn but up.

So I began to pray to Jesus. I started to sob and weep so uncontrollably that my eyes were swollen. I prayed to Jesus, asking, "Jesus, please forgive me all of my sins, for backsliding and making a complete mess of my life and for leaving my two young boys to fend for themselves while I moved away to party." I continued to pray, "Jesus, please forgive me for being so disobedient, and remove this horrible drug addiction from me," and I thanked him for taking care of me even when I was bad. I prayed, "Jesus, I love you, and I will never turn away from you again as long as live." And I meant this with every fiber of my being.

My last prayer was for my son, Adrian. I asked, "Father, please send a guardian angel to watch over my son, Adrian, who was stationed in Japan and due to ship out to Iraq." I continued, "Jesus, please don't allow my son to go to Iraq, because he is legally blind in one eye, and he won't make it over there. Please bring him home safe to me," In Jesus' name I prayed, "Amen."

You won't believe it, but the very next evening, my son called from Japan, and the very first words out of his mouth were, "Mom, I think I have a guardian angel, because I am not going to Iraq after all. I am being dismissed with a medical discharge, and I will be coming home." When I heard this, it literally gave me goose bumps over my entire body because it was total confirmation that Jesus had heard my prayers and had not only forgiven me but was bringing my son home as I had asked.

The reason I knew this was a message from God is because the only one who knew about this request for a guardian angel was Jesus. So Jesus answered me through my son.

I was so overjoyed with relief that I cannot express in words how I felt inside. I honestly did not think that Jesus would ever forgive me for all the bad things I had done. Especially after I had asked Jesus to come into my heart and have received the Holy Spirit at age nine, so I knew that what I was doing was wrong and kept doing it.

It made me sick to realize that I had wasted all of those years sinning when I should have been serving the Lord. But now I know that our God is merciful, loving, and forgiving. *Praise God for that!*

It was after this confirmation that I understood what Janet meant when she said to me before she moved, ***"Marla, no matter what happens in your life, you will always know your way back home."*** She was so right, because once you have given your life to Christ, you are stamped as his. And once you feel his loving presence inside you, you will always know your way back home, even if you stray. **Praise the Lord Almighty.**

17. My Promise to God

After my son called and I had confirmation that I had been forgiven for everything, I felt like a completely different person. When I woke up the next morning—I am not kidding you—the addiction was gone. I felt happy and completely at peace because I knew the Lord was going to take care of me from now on. I started listening to that gut feeling, which is the Holy Spirit, and it was telling me I needed to put myself into a rehab facility to clean out. I cut off all ties with old friends I had drug connections with and called a recovery house to put my name on the list for a room. This facility was free for individuals who did not have any income, and this was the perfect description of me!

With the little bit of money I had managed to save, I rented a small storage space and began to clean out my personal belongings from the motor home, so I would be ready to move when the room was ready. I had also purchased an older used Honda and was not sure where I was going to store it while I was in the program, because no vehicles were allowed there.

Finally, one Saturday morning around 10:00, the recovery house called. They said, "We have an available room, but you need to be here today by 1:30 p.m. to claim it." This was such short notice.

So I called my son, Evan, to help me. We contacted my ex-husband, and he agreed to take the motor home and park it on his property. My son drove it over to his property, so that was one obstacle out of the way. But now I had to find a place to park my Honda.

Evan followed me in his car to the storage facility to see if they had any spaces available, but there weren't any. Evan and I just sat in our cars and stared at each other with hopelessness. We did not know what else to do. I could not take my car to the rehab facility, because they would not allow it. At this point, I was in real trouble, because I had given the motor home to my ex-husband, which basically left me homeless. We did not know what to do.

We heard a woman's voice coming from inside the storage office, yelling, "Hey, a space for your car just opened up, and you can have it." Evan and I just looked at each other in complete amazement. Again we saw our amazing God in action and could not believe our eyes. So I parked the car in the space, and Evan proceeded to drive me to Seaside. We had twenty-five minutes to get there, so we drove rather fast, but I got there with five minutes to spare.

I spent thirty days in this program, because **I** needed to make sure that I was strong enough to fight off Satan's temptations **with the drugs** and I needed a place to live. **But** I think that the most important reason that the Lord sent me there was to share my testimonies on how God had answered my prayers and **to** encourage others.

18. A Miracle for My Friend

One particular lady in the program named Linda seemed very interested in God and wanted to study the Bible with me. Linda shared with me one day that she wanted to see her eight-month-old grandson, but the caseworker did not like her because of her drug problems and would not allow it. Linda came to me, crying and totally distraught. She wanted to see her grandson desperately, and they kept telling her no. So I said, "Let's start praying to God that he will change the caseworker's mind."

Well, God did it again; the very next morning, the caseworker called and said, "I am going to allow you to see your grandson today and will bring him by to visit with you, but it will only be for a half hour."

Linda could not believe it. She was overjoyed and said to me, "God is real, and I totally believe in him now."

Again I was in total awe at the amazing power of our God. You may not be able to see him or touch him, but you can feel his love, and you can watch him do what you think is impossible. *God is real and he lives.*

18. Taking a Step in Faith

It wasn't long before I knew it was time to leave this facility. The main reason was because we had to have prayer meetings in secret. The name "Jesus" was not allowed. You could only refer to Jesus as "Higher Power," and this just didn't work for me. So I called the only one who had stood by me through everything I had been through, and that was my son, Evan. I asked him, "Evan, bring my suitcases, and plan on helping me move out when you come to visit this Sunday."

Evan said, "Mom, are you sure? Where are you going to go? You have nowhere to live."

I said, "I don't know where I will live, but I know that I am not supposed to be here any longer."

So Evan came and picked me up. When the lady in the office saw that I was packing the car with my suitcases, she yelled out, "Hey, you can't just leave!" and I said," Yes, I can, because I placed myself here. I was not court ordered like the others."

The office lady said, "I am going to call the manager."

I said, "Go ahead."

Then she yelled out again, "You can't leave until you have experienced the miracle."

I replied, "You mean Jesus Christ? Well, his Spirit lives in me and has been with me all along, and I just haven't been listening to him, so yes, I have experienced this *miracle*."

Evan and I continued to load my suitcases into the car. We were just about ready to drive off when one young man who had just arrived at the program the day before came up to me and said, "You are going to make out there, I just know it, because being around you is like being around kindness."

I said, "Thank you." As we drove off, I said to Evan, "I feel so honored at what that young man said to me because I think that he can feel the warm love of Jesus Christ radiating out from me."

While Evan was driving me to Watsonville, he asked me, "Mom, where are you going to live?"

I said, "I am not sure, but I trust that God will provide that for me when we get to Watsonville."

As soon as we got there, Evan said, "Let's go to the car wash, because this car is filthy."

I said, "Okay."

As soon as we drove into the car wash, we both spotted my brother and his son. They were washing his work truck. "Hi, Jim," I said. "How are you doing?"

He said, "Good, what about you?"

I said, " I am doing okay. I just got out of the rehab facility house, and I am going to have to try to find a place to live. Hopefully the Salvation Army has a room."

Jim said, "Hey, we need someone to babysit our son while my wife and I work. Do you think you would be interested in staying with us?"

I could not believe my ears. I said, "Yes, of course I would, but please make sure that is okay with your wife first."

Jim said, "Okay, then I will call you later to let you know what my wife says."

Jim did not call me back right away, so I had to use the only credit card that was not maxed out and got a room at a hotel for the night. Evan took me to get my Honda out of storage and back to the room to help carry my suitcases upstairs. Evan said, "Mom, I need to run some errands, but I will be back to spend the night with you."

I said, "That is fine."

It was around 6:30 p.m., and I still had not heard from Jim, so I decided to go to an AA meeting. After the meeting, I returned to the hotel to find Jim and Evan waiting for me in the parking lot. My brother asked, "Where have you been? You are not doing drugs again, are you?"

I said, "Of course not. I went to an AA meeting, Jim. Please believe me that I will never go backwards again, and I mean it."

Evan chuckled and said, "See, Jim, I told you that Mom was probably at an AA meeting, and I was right."

Jim had come to tell me his wife had agreed to let me stay with them. I was very happy.

Do you see how amazing God is? He does provide you with everything you need. This was not luck or coincidence that I met up with my brother at the car wash and that he would ask me to live with him. This was God in action again! He is so amazing.

You really don't know what God's purpose is when you go through trials, but he plans everything to work out perfectly. Sometimes things happen at the last minute, but they always happen right on time.

19. First Job from God

I lived with Jim and his wife for about a year, and within that year, I re-earned the trust of my entire family. They could see the change in me that Jesus was doing.

Living only on what I had saved and having no other source of income, I cleaned house, did all the laundry, cooked for the entire family, and babysat in lieu of paying rent. This went on for about six months, until I realized that I needed a job, so I applied at a large retail chain in Salinas.

I remember being the last customer one Friday night, sitting at a computer filling out an online application. It was 11:30 p.m., and a lady said, "You are going to have to finish up now, because we are closing the doors."

I said, "I just finished."

Two weeks later, I got a call to come in for an interview.

When I got there, I interviewed with the supervisor for the boys' department and she said, "You are sure lucky, because you were the very last person that we accepted and hired for the December openings." She hired me, and I was scheduled to start three days before Thanksgiving.

Again you can see that this wasn't luck. God had his hand in this too!

20. God Removes Obstacles

I started my new job as a floor associate in the boys' department on November 21, 2004. This was very physically hard, because you were on your feet all day and always cleaning up after rude people. I usually worked the entire weekend and had Mondays, Tuesdays, and Wednesdays off.

When I took my breaks I would try to keep to myself, but could not help but overhear gossip, so I tried to stay clear of it.

One day in the break-room I made the mistake of mentioning to Sue that I was a Christian. When she asked what religion, I said, "Pentecostal."

She said, "Oh no, Pentecostals are holy rollers and some pretty weird people. So that is why you keep to yourself. You must think you're better than everyone else." She continued, "I hate people like you who think they are Goody Two-Shoes."

Boy, disclosing this information was the worst thing I could have ever done, because she started vicious rumors about me and made working around her miserable.

Every night when I got home, I would pray, "Lord, please remove this lady and her supervisor from my path and expose them for the type of people they are."

It was a Thursday, the first day of my work-week, so I headed toward the break room to clock in. I did not see that lady or her supervisor and wondered where they were, because they were usually the first two people I would run into.

I asked my supervisor where they were, and she said, "Oh, they were caught having intimate relations in his car last night out in the parking lot, and they were both fired on the spot."

This was amazing to me. The Lord removed both of these horrible people from my life just like that! I did not have to do anything except give my problem to God.

You can trust him with every *little* thing in your life, because Jesus wants that one-on-one personal relationship with you. So another prayer was answered.

21. Second Job Was not in God's Plan

Almost a year had gone by, and I was still living with my brother and his wife. I was not able to help with the household chores as before, because of the job. I was working from 3:30 p.m. to 11:30 p.m., and this left me literally exhausted and too tired to keep up the household chores that I had been doing for them.

This started causing friction, so they both decided that I needed to start paying rent for the room. I agreed with this, because it only seemed fair; however, they wanted me to pay $600 a month, and I was only making $800 a month. This was almost my whole check, and it wasn't going to allow me to save any money for my own place. I was not sure what to do.

Then my brother Robert asked me if I wanted to move in with him. He said, "I will not charge you any rent as long as you take a class in real estate, so you can get your license, sell homes, and get back on your feet." I agreed and moved in with them in November 2005.

I continued to work for this retail chain and took classes in the evening to obtain my real estate license. I finished my real estate classes, took the exam, and passed. I wanted to start working strictly for a real estate firm to learn the business. So when my job started forcing me to work at the cash register without an increase in pay, I quit.

Luckily I found a real estate office in Salinas that agreed to train me. I purchased my business cards and reported every day. After I learned that I would have to pay for my desk, phone, fax machine, chair, etc., I realized that I was not going to be able to afford to even get started in this business. I sure wish I had known all of this in the beginning.

When the housing market took an immediate turn for the worse and became a buyer's market, I had no choice but to quit and start looking for job that pays. You do not make any money unless you sell a house, so I could not continue.

When you are not on the path that God wants you on, he will close the door. So as far as this path went, he not only closed the door, he locked it.

There I was, unemployed, and I had burned my bridge at the other job because I did not give them two weeks' notice. And to make matters worse, I did not qualify for unemployment benefits, because I quit. So I really blew it.

22. God Points Me to Job Number 3

Several months passed and I kept applying for job after job with no luck whatsoever. One day while driving to Watsonville to look for work, something inside me said, "Go back and apply for a job at the company that you had worked for two years ago." So I made that right turn and headed to a sanitation company out in the country.

When I pulled up to their house and got out of the car, the owners came out of their house and saw that it was me and said, "Well, I can't believe it," and "How have you been?"

I said, "Pretty good," and continued, "Hey, I am looking for work and just wanted to know if you had any openings."

Sandy said, "What a coincidence, because our secretary just quit yesterday, and we need someone as soon as possible."

"Wow," I said, "this is great news because I can start tomorrow if you want me to."

Sue said, "Absolutely. Be here at 8:00 a.m."

So here it is again! This was no coincidence. It was another blessing sent to me from God.

23. God Provides Me with an Apartment

In the midst of all this, my Adrian had come home from the marines and was staying in that filthy motor home parked at my ex-husband's house. I knew that this motor home had horrible living conditions, because I once lived in it myself. It had fleas and ticks embedded into the carpet from the dog I once had. It was freezing at night and had no hot running water. I had to find a way to get an apartment large enough for both of us fast, so I started looking in the newspaper.

Finally after two months of diligently searching I found one. It was one-bedroom for only $725.00 a month. I knew I could afford that now with the income I would be receiving from this new job, so I applied for it. It is so funny, because my brother's wife said to me, "Marla, your credit is shot; you not will not be able to qualify to rent *any* apartment."

I said, "Well, I have to try."

I carefully typed up a nice letter and sent it to the landlord, explaining to him, "My credit may have problems, but I would like to be given a chance to prove that I am dependable." I said, "I can give you three months' rent in advance if you will just give me this chance and trust me." I submitted the application and the letter to the landlord and waited for him to call me with either a yes or no.

On September 15, 2005, while I was sitting on the patio at my brother's house, the call came in. It was the landlord, and he said,

"Marla, I am going to let you have this apartment and trust your word that you will be able to make the payments." He continued, "You do not have to give me the three months in advance; just the first month will be fine."

I could not believe it. I hung up the phone and looked over at my sister-in-law and said, "I got it."

She said, "You mean he actually rented the apartment to you, even with your bad credit?"

I said, "Yes." She just sat there in total amazement.

When my brother heard this, he was also amazed and said, "I'll help you move and even give you some furniture to start out with."

I rented this apartment sight unseen because I just knew that God had sent it to me.

So on October 1, 2005, I moved to Watsonville. When I got to the front door, I was shocked, because it had a picture on the window that said "Hawaii," and this is the exact same emblem that I had on the ornament hanging on my keychain. Seeing this, I knew that this apartment was for me and that God sent it.

24. My Sons Forgive Me

The first Saturday in October 2005, I moved into the small one-bedroom apartment located in downtown Watsonville. To me it was perfect compared to living in that flea- infested motor home. It had an extremely tiny kitchen, one small bedroom, a small bathroom with a shower stall only, and a rather large living room, but most importantly to me, it had electricity, a refrigerator, and hot running water.

I felt blessed and could not ask for more. So many of us take for granted the simple things that the Lord provides us, and we forget to give thanks for them. Now that I know how miserable it is to live without them, I will never forget to give thanks for these basic things again. I can truly say that I know exactly how homeless people feel.

Even before I was completely settled in, I called my son, Adrian, and said, "Please come live with me; the small bedroom is yours." My son came by to see the apartment and seemed like he was apprehensive to make the move.

I explained to him, "Honey, you can trust me. Jesus has changed my life, and I will never go backwards again." I continued, "Now that I am back with Jesus, I am staying on I-5 all the way now; no exits for me, so please come live with me."

Finally Adrian said, "Okay," and Evan helped him move in.

Adrian and I started to become closer after he moved in. He slowly began to forgive me for leaving both him and Evan stranded after the sale of the first house. Evan was only seventeen years old, and Adrian had just turned eighteen. So they were on their own, and this just wasn't fair.

I encouraged Adrian to come to church with me on Sunday, but I never pushed it, because I knew Jesus would grab him when his heart is ready. What I would do is discuss the Scriptures that were discussed in church each Sunday. Most of the time, it would trigger him to search them out in his own Bible, and that was good. Evan began to forgive me as well, and when he came to visit us from L.A., we would all sit and discuss Scriptures.

When Adrian moved in with me, he had a job with a construction company. It only paid minimum wage, so he was searching for something better. Finally he landed a job working with my son-in-law's boss. This went okay for a while, but I noticed that he would come home stressed and very unhappy.

It was around this time that Adrian was severely beaten in the parking lot where we lived. His jaw was broken in two places, and according to the emergency doctors, it was truly a miracle that he even survived at all. Because he had to have his mouth wired shut, he was unable to work during this healing period, so the company laid him off.

After the wires were removed, Adrian found another job working in a warehouse. He seemed pretty happy, and this job lasted about eight months until he quit because he wanted to find a job that paid better. He began the job search again.

In the next year or so, Adrian found numerous jobs with temp agencies, but they would never last more than two months. At this point, I began to realize that he was having trouble keeping any job—period!

I did not realize that the learning disability he had been diagnosed with as a child would affect him so significantly as an adult. I kept encouraging him by saying, "Honey, God knows you have this disability, and you may not believe right now, but God will turn it around and make good come out of it someday!"

25. God Always Answers Prayers

Around this same time, I learned that Adrian was up to his neck in debt. He had kept it hidden from me out of embarrassment, but once I learned how much he owed to his creditors, I knew that bankruptcy was unavoidable.

So I helped him file for bankruptcy. We thought he would at least be able to keep up the payments with the 2000 Honda that he purchased, so we did not list it as one of the items to go back. However, he soon began to fall behind on the car payments, and we were stuck trying to come up with the money for late payment fees that were building up.

I decided to contact the bank and have them come and pick up the car, but they wouldn't. They wanted their money, not the car. So I went to my bank and transferred the loan into my name. As soon as that was complete, I began spreading the word that I wanted to sell the car. With my job about to end and the first payment coming up, I didn't know what I was going to do.

After church, the Sunday before that payment was due, I sat in the car and began to pray. "Lord, please send me a buyer for this car, so that I will not even have to come up with the first payment." I drove to my brother's house in Salinas, so that he could take pictures and advertise it on Craigslist.

We took the pictures, and my brother had just barely listed them up on the Web when the phone rang. It was a co-worker, letting me know that she wanted the car because the engine in her husband's truck blew up last night.

I just could not believe my ears. I told my brother what she said, and he could not believe it either. I met the co-worker at the bank on Monday. The car loan was transferred into her name. Just like that, I was out of debt, my son's name was cleared, the bank was happy, and my co-worker had a good car! **What a win-win situation!**

Only the Lord could pull off something like this so perfectly. God heard my prayer and answered this one immediately. He is so amazing!

26. God Turns Bad into Good

Adrian was still struggling trying to find a job, and I would tell him that he just needed to pray to God for a job and have faith that he will provide one. He would just get angry and say, "I pray to God for a good job, but he isn't listening to me because nothing is happening."

I said, "Honey if you haven't asked Jesus to forgive you of your sins and to come into your heart, your prayers aren't getting through to God," I continued, "You have to pray to Jesus, and he takes your prayers to the Father." Then I quoted a Scripture directly from the Bible where it says in **John 14:6,** *"I am the way, the truth, and the life. No one comes to the Father except through me."*

So I continued, "If you have been praying directly to God and not to Jesus, then God has not heard your prayers, and that is why you are not getting any answers." Adrian just looked at me, and I could tell that he understood what he needed to do. It was not long after this that he really began to read and study the Bible diligently. I truly believe he did ask Jesus to come into his heart because things started to turn around for him.

With God's help, Adrian qualified for assistance through the Educational Rehabilitation Program, and this led him to a good job that he likes. He has been there for over a year now, and they absolutely love him. And what is more amazing is that because they hired him knowing that he has this disability, they can't just fire him without good cause. So I told Adrian, "See, God took this learning disability, which you thought was bad, and made good come out of it." Adrian just looked at me and said, "I know."

(Romans 8:28) *"And we know that all things work together for good to those who love God, to those who are called according to his purpose."*

While Adrian had been struggling with his job issues, I was too. This mom-and-pop septic company that I was working for had horrible working conditions. The office was on their property, and it was a remodeled horse stall. The bathroom facilities consisted of an outhouse located about six feet from the office with no running water. Most people would not even consider working in this type of environment, but I needed this job in order to support Adrian and myself, so I didn't care.

The only thing that became unbearable was the daily verbal abuse from the alcoholic husband. I would bite my tongue and keep my hurt feelings to myself, but after a year of this, I couldn't take it any longer.

I spoke with the wife of this company, because she was very nice, and explained, "I need to look for a job that offered me a future."

She said, "I am sorry to see you go, but I understand, and I will write you a letter of recommendation to help you." She continued, "You can keep working for us until something else comes along."

27. I Am Right Where God Wants Me to Be

After about three weeks of diligently searching, I found a temporary job with a very reputable company in Watsonville. I was so excited about this, I called my brother to let him know the good news. My brother said, "That is great, because when you become permanent, you will have retirement, medical, and dental benefits."

But my sister-in-law said, "You might as well forget it, because they only hire Hispanics."

I said, "Well, I am going to try anyway and trust in God."

Unfortunately, I misunderstood when I took this new job and quit the septic company that it was an on-call and part-time position. So here I was, working approximately twelve hours per month, and this was just not going to cut it. I needed more money to make the monthly rent.

So I began to pray to Jesus for help. One afternoon, while I was sitting in the apartment feeling depressed and wondering what I was going to do, the phone rang. It was this same company I had the part-time job with. They called to offer me a temporary office position, which was eight hours a day, five days a week and would last three months. Before the lady could even finish explaining the job duties to me, I said, "Yes, I will take the job."

So I started this position in March of 2006. I felt like I had died and gone to heaven. This boss was so kind and understanding that I had to pinch myself to make sure it wasn't a dream. I learned some new office skills, but my main duty was to place orders. I enjoyed this and felt really comfortable doing this type of work, because I had been a planner, and ordering and coordinating the delivery of products was my expertise.

Everything was going great, but June was approaching quickly. I began to worry about how I was going to be able pay the rent again. So I prayed to Jesus for help. What I did not expect was to have this job extended indefinitely, because the woman who was out on medical leave was not coming back. So I did not lose my job in June as scheduled. I could not believe it—my prayers were answered again! I was going to be able to keep working in this position and was very grateful for this. But unfortunately, I found out that my boss was going to retire in June, and I was concerned about who would be replacing her.

June 30 came, and my boss retired. I felt very sad but kept plugging away at placing the orders. From July to August, I worked independently and completely unsupervised, but this did not bother me, because I was used to it. Then on August 1, my new boss was hired.

28. God Shows His Awesome Power for All to See

For the last four years that I have worked at this job, it has been one trial after another. I have had five different bosses. My position has been eliminated three times and once taken from me by someone with more seniority. But each time I was supposed to be laid off or moved from this department, God has intervened, and the decision was reversed so that I have been able to keep this same position.

I know that certain individuals wanted me to lose my job, and they thought that it was a slam-dunk that I would be gone, but they were no match for God's power. When you are on the path God wants you to be on, *no one* can interfere with it. **No one**! So each time I went down to HR to lose my job and I ended up keeping it, they could see that it was God because of the unique way he did it. He changed the minds of the people making the layoff decisions, and this just didn't normally happen. God made it very obvious that he was in control. Right now I am working in the same position that the Lord gave me back in September 2006, and I have enjoyed working with all of my co-workers.

But now, with continual budget cuts and the rumor of job layoffs, the atmosphere has become very hostile and cutthroat again. I am praying for God's protection in all of this mess and to provide me with another job if this one ends, but "thy will be done." God knows what is best for me, and I trust that he will open another door if this one closes.

Well, God did it again. He provided me with another position within this company, and I am very blessed. The way I view this move to the new position is that this is a re-assignment from the heavenly Father. I have other people he wants me to share my testimonies with, and I will do so with great pleasure. I want God, my Father, to be proud of me when he looks down from heaven and says, "Well done, my faithful servant."

29. What I Have Learned through All These Trials

In closing, I must say that all my testimonies are true, and every trial that I have had to experience has taught me to trust in God completely. I trust him for every little thing that I need. I know that He will answer every prayer, so I remain patient and wait for his answer. But I think that *the most important thing of all* is to *thank God* for *every single blessing he gives you. Don't ever take them for granted.*

Sometimes God answers your prayers with a **"no,"** sometimes with a **"yes,"** and sometimes it seems to take forever for any kind of answer, but God will *always* answer them. But it is in his timing, not ours.

Sometimes when the Lord answers your prayers, it is awesome because he does it in such a *big* way that everyone who is watching sees it and knows that there is no other explanation, except that *God does exist!*

My faith has been strengthened because of everything that has happened to me, and I would not trade it for anything in the world.

It has brought me closer to him than I have ever been in my life, and I have been very blessed and fortunate to actually see *God* in action. I can truly say right now in my life that I don't just love God; I am *"in love"* with God and Jesus. I find myself not wanting to talk about anything else but them, and I try to think the way he would think, so I don't do anything that would hurt their feelings. To me, God is my Father, and I am his daughter.

(2 Corinthians 6:18) *"I will be a Father to you, And you shall be MY sons and Daughters, Says the Lord Almighty."*

So I want to tell everyone that *"**Nothing is impossible with God.** He can make happen what others say is impossible because he is the Almighty **God.**"*

Until part two, I am closing for now, and I hope and pray that everyone who reads my testimony is touched somehow and will consider asking Jesus to come into his or her heart.

> *May God bless and keep you safe always.*
> —*Marla Almaraz*

"You don't want to be caught dead without Jesus."

Job Opportunities

We are recruiting individuals who are interested in serving the Lord—now and in the future "Kingdom of God," which is coming soon!

No experience needed, will train.

Benefits include:

- A one-on-one" personal relationship with your **Creator.**
- A boss that truly loves and cares about you!
- 24/7 protection from your enemies by ***God*** himself!
- Peace of mind and true happiness.
- No layoffs—job is permanent, lasts forever, even after death, it's forever! ***"Eternal."***

Please feel free to come join me and learn more! It is all the in Holy Bible.